.... And Then We Moved To Royal Quays

'**.... And then we moved to Royal Quays**' is the result of North Tyneside Libraries Reminiscence sessions which took place at the Royal Quays Community Centre during the latter part of 1994.

The memories were provided by the 'Ladies of the Royal Quays'.

Marjorie Culyer, Helen Ferry, Kathy Johnson, Eunice Kerrigan, Betty Lacey, Joyce Miller, Eileen Ruddle, Hannah Sullivan, Lily Watson, Pat Watson and Margaret Wiseman

to whom our grateful thanks are extended.

Funding was provided by the Tyne and Wear Development Corporation with enthusiastic support from the staff at the Royal Quays Education Centre.

This project will be of benefit to the whole community, both now and in years to come, and provided enormous enjoyment to those involved.

Val White
Diane Leggett
December 1994

ISBN 0 906 529 20 4

© North Tyneside Libraries
North Shields
1995

Earliest Memories

I was born in Sidney Street - a basement flat - below the grating. Then we had a flat - 47 Scorer Street - We overlooked the park and the park keeper, Mr. Crow used to give us half an orange each for sweeping out his hut. The flat had a toilet on the veranda outside - the toilet floor had to be scrubbed with a pumice stone to keep it yellow. In the poor weather, I played with my dolls on the floor and my friend and I used to talk to each other over our metal veranda rails. We had a scullery and a bath under the bench. We had two bedrooms, one for mother and father and the four girls in the other. The bedrooms had brass bedsteads with knobs which unscrewed and you could hide things inside them.(e.g. chewing gum) My eldest sister, Molly, had a single bed and the two others had a double bed. I had to sleep between them either at the top or the bottom of the bed, and I was either kicked or squashed.

One of my earliest memories was sitting in my pram while my mother was standing talking to Mrs. Basillie for ages - I said "Shut up Bad Billy".

Starting school at 5 years old is my first memory - I was an only child so I was a spoiled brat. Father took me to the Quayside Market in Newcastle on a Sunday morning and bought me everything I asked for. The whole family went to Grandmas every Saturday night.

We were quite posh, we had a three bedroomed upstairs flat in Gerald Street, Wallsend. We had a living room and a scullery and as I was an only child, I had my own bedroom. The third bedroom was the spare room where all the junk was stored and before opening the front door, we had to close the spare room door to hide the mess.

My job was to wash the back stairs on a Saturday night. We had no electricity, only gas lighting, but we had running water. On a Friday night we had a tin bath in front of the fire, but we had a big scullery with a stone floor. The downstairs flat had an outside toilet and there were six children in the family. I always remember one of them shouting "bring some paper!". Toilet paper was newspaper squares. It was the children's job to cut the papers into squares and thread them onto a string. (Newsprint didn't rub off in those days!) Our flat overlooked the shipyards on one side and the railway line on the other.

My father worked at Swans and we could see all the ships being launched. If there was a special launch, father used to take us into the yard to see, and people used to come from miles around to watch, but we took them for granted when we could watch them all from the window anyway.

We moved to the house in the Ridges when I was 4 years old and my brothers and sisters chased up and down the stairs and through all the upstairs rooms with excitement. It had four bedrooms, a kitchen, scullery and bathroom, and a living room.

We lived at 2 Bellevue Terrace, Coach Lane, then 29 Railway Terrace. There was just my brother and myself and so we had our own bedrooms. I got rheumatic fever and had to be kept in the sitting room and so my brother moved into my bedroom. We had an outside toilet and the bath was underneath the bench in the scullery. Friday night was bath night. We had our own jobs and mine was to stone the floor with pumice. We went to school through the 'halfpenny hatch' from Railway Terrace to Queen Victoria School. I didn't want to go to school so I ran away into the park four times and Mr. Buck, the park keeper took me back and gave me a bunch of daisies. Mr. Buck never told my mother I had run away from school, and I couldn't take the daisies home or she would have found me out.

She told us to pretend to cry when we got there and she left us all in the office with Mr. Dyball, who worked there, telling him to look after us, as she had no money to feed us. The police came and by this time we were all screaming thinking that mother wasn't going to come back for us, except my oldest brother, who was still pretending to cry.

70 years ago, when I was about 5 years old, my father was ill and in those days a guardian's relief pension was paid weekly to feed the family while the father was unable to work. The two eldest children had left home, but that still left 10 children. Because my father refused to go into hospital (it was more of a workhouse than a hospital), the relief money was stopped. My mother took all of the children including the baby to the payment office in Willington Quay. She told us to pretend to cry when we got there and she left us all in the office with Mr. Dyball, who worked there, telling him to look after us, as she had no money to feed us. The police came and by this time we were all screaming thinking that mother wasn't going to come back for us, except my oldest brother, who was still pretending to cry. The police went to our house and my parents told them that they were burning empty boxes to keep warm.

We were picked up from the office eventually and my mother was given a voucher to buy food. We must have hated Mr. Dyball to remember his name after all these years. Father always suffered ill health and died aged 57 years. Mother lived to 83 years.

We lived on the Quay Main Street - 12 Union Road, Lowlights. There was a long dark alleyway with a big yard on the right and houses on the left. The front door opened onto the living room which we called the kitchen - it had an old black range, a big table, a settee and a desk-bed (which the oldest lad slept in) The desk-bed was like a high sideboard - the doors opened and the bed pulled down - the bedclothes were kept inside it like a cupboard. There were 13 children - the oldest, Sarah, was married and had left home - The rest of the children slept in three beds in one small room. I slept in a cot in my parents small bedroom until I was six years old, because there was no room for me anywhere else. We had gas only and a tap and a toilet outside in the yard. There was a boarded up dark passage which we were told, had used to be used to hide Whisky brought round the Tynemouth Middens to the Quay. It was a very old house, but it was always a happy house.

Most of the houses had lino or canvas on the floor with clippie mats. The walls were painted - some had flowered wallpaper. The border was often taken carefully off the wall and put into another room when we redecorated. The wallpaper was taken up to the furniture, but not behind it, so that when you moved house, several different patterns could be seen in each room where the furniture had been moved.

There was usually a large table, scrubbed white, a desk-bed, wooden chairs with arms and crackets (or fireside stools with lids) - only the bare essentials. The walls were rotten and there were bugs behind the paper by the time the houses were pulled down. To kill the bugs the backs of the furniture were painted with Blue Umption, or pots of beer were left to catch them in. Mother washed in the wash-house, sometimes as late as six in the evening. She washed for the fort officers. She got 2d per shirt, 1d per towel and a halfpenny for 6 handkerchiefs. There was a fire under the wash-tub, where she possed and scrubbed the laundry, then dolly-blued and starched it, then flat-ironed it dry. She spat on the iron to see if it was hot enough.

The morgue for drowned sailors was in Coach Lane and was known as the 'Dead House'. Old Lizzie Griggs hosed down the bodies and Meggie Palmer laid them out for a payment of 10/- per body from Turnbulls.

I remember that 50 Preston Road was the Workhouse in North Shields. It had stone floors and settles in rows. All the men wore dark suits. There was a man who sat and sketched landscapes, buildings and animals and the children sat and watched him.

He was stuck in the tub with his cap over his eyes and his legs dangling over the side, soaked to the skin. We dared to laugh at him and he replied: "That'll be ten bob off this suit at the pawnshop on Monday!"

We were bathed on a Saturday Night in front of a roaring fire. My sister Eileen was bathed first and I was in the tub when my father came home very drunk. He was dressed in a dark suit and a grey cap and as soon as he came in he started shouting at my mother. She lost her temper and pushed him and he fell into the tub. He was stuck in the tub with his cap over his eyes and his legs dangling over the side, soaked to the skin. We dared to laugh at him and he replied: "That'll be ten bob off this suit at the pawnshop on Monday!" The suit was put into the pawn shop on a Monday morning to buy food and we had to run round to get it back on a Friday afternoon. Graham's Pawn Shop was in Stephenson Street and Fisher's was in Church Way, there was also one called Driver's and another in Prudhoe Street.

One hot summer's day I climbed under my mother's bed and fell asleep on the cool canvas floor. The family and the police were out all day looking for me. Another time, the search party was on for me and I had fallen asleep on the beach. When they found me the tide was coming in and the water had nearly covered me. I was always going missing, and had usually fallen asleep somewhere.

I remember going to nursery school on Howdon Road. I was about 3 or 4 years old and I hated it. I played with an older girl who lived in Bedford Street above the Tiger Stairs and I used to run away from home to go to the fish quay with her. I came back filthy and smelling of fish and that's why I was made to go into the nursery school. They made us sleep on camp beds with grey army blankets in the afternoon and I didn't want to go to sleep. From nursery I was sent to St Cuthbert's School, we had outside toilets and it was next to the convent. As we passed the convent we were made to cross ourselves, as the school was strict Catholic. We were embarrassed to be seen doing this, but we were afraid not to.

We used to amuse ourselves by playing with buttons on the pavements when we were kids - you had to throw the buttons into a chalk square. Everyone cut the buttons off garments before throwing them away.

Staggy the Ironmonger had a place in Howard Street - it burned down - I remember watching the fire. He was a rag and bone man - he would take away anything you gave him. He had a fire going all the time and burnt the rubbish - sometimes it smelled terrible.

There were cafes down the alleyways off Clive Street. It was the Mediterranean Quarter of North Shields. There were a lot of Maltese, Greek and Spanish people living in that area. The Barber was Joe Lois - a Spaniard.

My father went to sea and my mother had to go to the shipping office to collect his pay. My dad's Union dues had to be paid at the Seaman's Union Hut, we went that way to pay the Warren's bill, too. We remember the Steam Ferry as the Penny Ferry - as the fare was only a penny. There was also the "Halfpenny Dodger".

Wakefield, who is now the funeral director, was the Charabanc owner. We went on day trips. Even though they were very overcrowded we were really happy going on the charabanc trips. We went to Greggs Coffee Shop for lunch when we worked at Tyne Brand Factory. There was a hut on top of Ballast Hill, Dock Road. It was from there that they fired the one o'clock gun.

6

Ralph Gardner's House, Chirton Cottage - The monument still stands. We used to steal apples from the gardens on the way to school. Thompsons was the Red Stamp Store. Red stamps were the forerunner of Green Shield Stamps - you saved them up to exchange for goods. Mrs. Winter, from Winters Store, was known as "Ganny Winters". She wore a black dress and a white pinny and had her hair in a bun. She sold Toffee Pats in greased sweet cases for halfpenny each from her door. Dr. Yates and then Dr. Philips had a dispensary and surgery for paying-patients at 6d per week fee.

My friend May Preston and I went to visit a fortune teller in Dockwray Square. She lived in a dark basement flat with a roaring fire and a crystal ball. We were scared of her, but she rightly told me that my brother would go on the stage and would die young.

Christmas Past

One Christmas, my father was on the sick from work and was not being paid. At school we were asked to put our names on a sheet of paper if our father was out of work. I wrote my name and address and thought no more about it until on Christmas Eve there was a knock at the door and the poor-cart had a present with my name on. Mum was so annoyed that I had brought shame to her door by telling people that we couldn't pay our way, but I got a great present. I was thrilled with it - it was a cardboard dolls house.

We went to bed very early on Christmas Eve. We awoke in the early hours on Christmas morning. We always got a new coat and a pair of shoes and a new penny and an apple and orange.

"SPAM" — is the registered trademark distinguishing the product manufactured exclusively by Geo. A. Hormel & Co. "Spam" is made of pure pork shoulder meat with ham meat added. "Spam" is sold ONLY in 12 oz. tins plainly marked with the trademark "Spam." We are sorry that during the war, supplies of "Spam" are restricted.

* "Spam" is a registered trademark

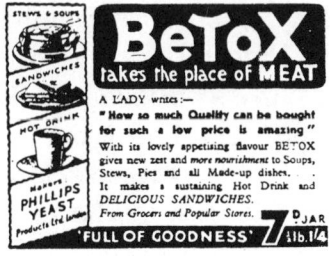

I remember one Christmas my two brothers were away in the services and one of them sent a record in a parcel. When my mother played the record on the wind-up gramophone, we all cried.

We never got a lot for Christmas, but what we got was appreciated. A lady my mum works for used to send us tins of sweets and biscuits.

We were told that if we didn't go to sleep that Father Christmas would leave no presents and we would only get a sock full of cinders or ashes.

We had a very big family and because we could not afford a Christmas Tree, we used to make a paper garland hung with sugar toys. We got a stocking with sweets, fruit, nuts and perhaps a little doll - but Christmas Day was a family day and we all enjoyed it. On New Years Eve the door was never locked, anyone could come in and join the family.

When my father got home from sea at Christmas time, he took me to Woolworths and got a little cradle with a white doll and a black doll. My brother and I got a desk and chair each on Christmas and it was just a little while ago when the desks were passed on to a Children's Home.

We spent Christmas Eve decorating the tree. I was an only child and so all our relatives and friends used to visit and bring me presents. There always seemed to be plenty to eat at Christmas time and loads of visitors at our house. I was sent to bed while the adults played cards. I was allowed to stay up until midnight on New Years Eve, but I could never get to sleep once I got to bed because the guests used to chat and listen to records until really late. Before Christmas, the whole house was cleaned from top to bottom. If any decorating had to be done it was done then. Everything in the house was gleaming and clean.

We had Chicken for Christmas Dinner, sometimes Pork or Rabbit as well. We didn't have Turkey - only posh people had Turkey!

We had Chicken for Christmas Dinner, sometimes Pork or Rabbit as well. We didn't have Turkey - only posh people had Turkey! We got to pull the wishbone. You had your stocking on the end of your bed, but your presents were left in the living room.

All the shops used to decorate their windows with toys and garlands. My mum couldn't afford a new doll for me and so a little girl gave me her old doll. Mum knitted new clothes for it and made it a new nose out of bread dough!

One year we got a lovely doll's house between us and it was our favourite toy. It was made by my brother and lasted for years. It had lights and hand-made furniture, and we played with it for hours. We had snakes and ladders and snap cards - playing cards were taboo in our house. My favourite was a nurse's uniform and doctor's bag.

School Days

I started Percy Main Council School aged 5 years in 1936. I went to Ralph Gardner at 11 years, but hated it. The headmistress at Percy Main was the only teacher I remember, I think she was called Miss Pigg. Ralph Gardner teachers were Miss Ord, Miss Russell, Miss Armstrong and Miss Johnson - she had a big bun in her hair and wore manly clothes. I liked science but didn't like history. I used to pick my hands to get the half day off to go to the Clinic in the Chase, but we used to go back to Betty Holland's house to make toffee while her mother was out at work.

I went to Queen Victoria School from 1937. I remember Miss Custard, Miss Davison and Mrs. Pearson. The headmistress at Queen Victoria was horrid, Miss Dowson. One teacher, Miss Murphy, kept my necklace for me during PE, and at the end of the lesson I went and asked for it to be returned. She chastised me for asking her, but would not return the necklace. My mother and grandmother went to school to see her about it but the necklace never came back. I went on to Weston Board School, but it was bombed during the war. I used to get sick in the Air Raid Shelter - I was terrified. We had a nice teacher called Miss Churnside, I liked her. After the bombing we were moved to Linskill. My favourite lessons were Painting and Sewing. I left school at 14 - I left on the Friday and started work in Hancocks Cake Shop on the following Monday morning. I wanted to learn to Type, but my mother said that wasn't a suitable job for a woman and I was made to go into the cake shop. I loved the job and still exchange Christmas and Birthday Cards with people from Hancocks.

I went to St. Bede's Catholic School when I was 5, from 1932 until I moved to East Howdon at age 13. I liked school but I remember hating one teacher called Miss McArdle. St. Aidan's in Willington Quay was a really friendly school and I liked it. I left at 14. The school day began with Catechism and then sums.

... and if we were naughty she used her pencil to poke you in the temple and said: "I'll knock you all the way to Jericho!" I got sick of this happening to me and boldly asked her where Jericho was - I was made to stand in the corner for the rest of the lesson.

I went to Addison Potter - one side of the school was for the infants and the other was for the girls. Then I transferred to Stephenson Memorial School in Howdon and then the new Stephenson School. Our sewing mistress was from Jarrow and if we were naughty she used her pencil to poke you in the temple and said: "I'll knock you all the way to Jericho!" I got sick of this happening to me and boldly asked her where Jericho was - I was made to stand in the corner for the rest of the lesson. We wore shoes with buttons and had to fasten them with a button hook. I liked Cookery and Poetry. We never got homework - only lines - and we were punished with a leather strap.

We went to Kettlewell School first, but I have no recollections of it, except that it was at the top of a very steep bank. We were sent to the Chase Open Air School when we got Scarlet Fever. I was about four and my sister Eileen was a year older.

At age 9, in about 1938 we moved to the Ridges and went to St. John's. I hated school, but we had fun going to school and coming home. I was a dunce when it came to Arithmetic. My brother Stan used to steal our milk money from us - he was two years older than us. We went to Ralph Gardner when we were 11 - the war was on then and when the sirens went you didn't know whether to run home or run to school. I remember Miss Ord the PE teacher. In sewing lessons I always got into trouble for tangling up yards of thread. Miss Johnson, the Science teacher was really scary - she wore a ginger hairy tweed suit and brogue shoes - she called us by our second names. I used to copy from the girl in front and she used to shout at me. If we dared to ask a question she used to bang her ruler down hard on the desk and make us jump.

I attended Carville School from 1935 until I was 14 years old, then I went on to study at Coulson's Commercial College, a Private College at the Green in Wallsend. I liked everything at school except for Geography, because I couldn't draw maps. We had a teacher who was like a Sergeant Major - but we found that she was very keen on Shakespeare. We used to ask her questions about Shakespeare plays to make her forget that she was supposed to be teaching PE or RI. She also taught us Rug-Making, which got us out of quite a few lessons. I failed my 11-plus exam so that I wouldn't have to go to High School, as they wore black stockings as part of the uniform - I hated black stockings! A wall separated the boys yard and the girls yard and when we took PE the boys used to jump up and look over the wall at us in our navy knickers!

My mother used to give me a penny to buy Walls Ice Cream from the Ice-Cream Seller's bicycle, but we never bought Ice Cream - we used to save it up and buy a packet of Woodbines to smoke at lunch times behind the toilet block.

Miss Blackburn was our Drama teacher, we were afraid of her as she used to single us out to stand up and read out parts in front of the class. My mother used to give me a penny to buy Walls Ice Cream from the Ice-Cream Seller's bicycle, but we never bought Ice Cream - we used to save it up and buy a packet of Woodbines to smoke at lunch times behind the toilet block. We paid someone, who didn't smoke, a penny - to be the lookout.

When I was about 13 years old, I went on holiday to Alston with my parents. I contracted Scarlet Fever and was sent to an isolation hospital in Longtown, near Carlisle. My parents had to go home without me and were distraught about leaving me behind, but I had a whale of a time. We were next door to an Air Force Base and were allowed to go for walks to get fresh air. We met a lot of Airmen. I was there for about 6 weeks and I loved it.

I started at Queen Victoria when I was about 5 years old and went to Ralph Gardner at 11 in 1944. Miss Atkinson was the cookery teacher and one day she caught me chewing gum. She told me to put the gum in the open fire, but it melted onto my finger and I couldn't get it off. I went to sit back in my place and she threw a pan at me, I ducked and it hit the girl behind. I had three older sisters and they were all better than me at school work - I had a hard time living up to them - I got sick of hearing "Why can't you be like your sister?" The best teacher I had was my first teacher at Queen Victoria - Miss Niven. On my first day, when playtime came I thought it was time to go home. My mother said it wasn't worth going back, but the next day I was frightened to go in case Miss Niven was cross with me. She took me by the hand and never mentioned the incident and I idolised her from that moment. She died shortly afterwards and we all got the day off school to attend her funeral.

We were forced to eat porridge for breakfast and made to eat Macaroni Cheese for dinner - it made me sick, but we had to force it down.

My most vivid memories are of the Open Air School. We were forced to eat porridge for breakfast and made to eat Macaroni Cheese for dinner - it made me sick, but we had to force it down. We had to go to bed after dinner in a shed with rows of camp-beds - we were woken from sleep to resume lessons in the afternoon, which made us bad-tempered and unable to work properly. We were very thin to start with, but you were taken there to build you up, which took some time for us! We were taken there by bus, which picked us up from home, and we had to stay there until we recovered.

I remember the Headmaster at St. John's School, Mr. Horne, he was a very fair man, but I didn't like school. I was always in trouble and given 50 lines for talking too much. Every report I got from school said on the bottom that I talked too much. I didn't like doing fractions - but the teacher used to mark my work right as she couldn't make out what I had written. At Ralph Gardner my favourite subjects were History and Geography.

I went to Meadow Well School until I was 7 and then Western until 11, then I went on to Ralph Gardner. Miss Ord became the headmistress. The best teacher at Ralph Gardner was "Ganny Lee" - but we didn't like Miss Liddle - she took us for Gardening and PE and made us go in the showers afterwards. I also left school on the Friday and started on the Monday Morning at Welch's Sweet Factory where I worked for 9 years.

I went to St. Joseph's Catholic School from Nursery School Age onwards - we were taught by Nuns who were very strict and we were afraid of them. I then went to St. Anselm's. I was caned by Miss Shippon, the Cookery teacher for smoking and skipping lessons. She used to catch your finger ends until they stung with the cane. My younger sister was very quiet at school and I was always compared to her - she used to tell my mother about my behaviour and I would get into trouble at home too.

We couldn't afford bus-fares so we had to walk from the bottom of the Ridges to St. Anselms. Miss Lownes the Science teacher used to throw the blackboard cleaning brush at us if we misbehaved, and Mr. Baines, the English master used to draw a chalk ring high up on the blackboard and make us stand on tiptoe with our nose pressed to the board inside the chalk ring until he allowed us to sit back in our seats, if he caught us talking in his class. The only teacher I liked was Mr. Dixon, as he used to give us matches to light our cigarettes at lunch times. We hid the cigarettes on the top of the high toilet cisterns - we were always being caught!

We always wore a white pinny under our coats for school.

The Miners Hall in Hawkey's Lane became the Boys Club. We all remember the open air baths and the park. We were made to go into the freezing cold water at the baths when we were taken by the school. It was so cold that we weren't able to learn to swim - I still can't!

Tynemouth Jubilee Infirmary became the Frater Maternity Home. Older people went to the workhouse instead of being taken to the hospital when they were ill. We were taken to the Isolation Hospital at Moor Park when we contracted Scarlet Fever as children. There were no houses around it then and even our mother was not allowed in to visit us.

Starting Work

I remember my last day at school. I hated it so much that I didn't go! At 14 years of age I left school and went to work in the Fish House on the Quayside. I'd always wanted to work here from being a child - I remember copying the Scottish Lasses who worked on the Quay, gutting and salting the herring, using a peg for a knife. The war was still on then. We had to wear "deckers" - a type of Wellington Boot, thick socks and black oil-skins, which were provided for us. Our hair was tied up in a turban. We were given the Herring by the Cran - which was four boxes. They were packed in ice and we had to split and gut them at a bench and then "pickle" them in the orange dye. They then had to be pricked on to long hooks on sticks and hung over troughs to dry in the kilns. We had to have our fingers and thumbs wrapped up as the hooks were sharp and caused cuts which became infected. The smoking rooms were long sheds with burning wood shavings dampened down with sand. The herring were hung on the racks and the poles were handed up to the "hanger". There was a certain way to twist the wrist to stop them from falling off. They were left overnight and then we packed them into boxes. We had to do all the lifting ourselves. The men did the fish and the women dealt with the kippers. I loved the job, the people were great to work with, and we got to travel around with the catches, according to the season. I worked from about 7.30am to 9pm and the wages were 7/6d per week.

When I worked with the herring we used to travel round with the catches and the changing seasons. I was working in the Isle of Man, when we had a visit from George Formby. He was a lovely man and immaculately dressed, but very down to earth. He came to talk to us all.

15

I loved my job on the Quay although the conditions were terrible and we always got poisoned hands. When there was a glut of herring we had to squeeze past the boxes to get to work. The Norwegian Herring were always packed in tons of ice and we worked knee-deep in the ice. We had tins of water on the benches to warm our hands, but most of the time you couldn't feel them. If you cut yourself, you didn't know about it until you put your hands in the water. We went home shattered, freezing and soaking wet, but I still loved the job. The only problems were that no-one would sit next to me on the bus because of the fishy smell, especially when we had been given the seconds to bring home. Our hands were dyed orange and we had to steep them in Rose-Water to try and soften them. I loved dancing, and we went to dances five nights a week, but often none of the boys would dance with us because of our rough, orange hands.

My first job was at the Lord Nelson Pub in Camden Street. I worked from 9 am to 10 pm - I can't remember how much I was paid, but the wages would have been quite poor. I was employed to look after the owners' children Patricia, aged 3 and Leslie aged 18 months. Their surname was Webb. I often took them to my mother's house to keep them occupied. Their mother, Peg was a very nice woman, I found the father very strict with the children. I got the job through my mother, who was the cleaner for the pub. I worked there for about 2 years. After that I went to the Tyne Brand Factory and then worked in the NAAFI when I was about 20. I met my husband there. After the war I worked in Wilkinson's Pop Factory in King Street.

I was 14 years old when I went into Service, recommended by the service agency who came into the Dole office. One of the servants who had married the boss was my employer. I had to live in as the post was in Winchester. I got the bus all by myself - I was terrified. I was travel sick on the bus and so I sat in my seat when everyone else got off at the stops on the way. When the driver got back on to set off again, he jammed my thumb in the door, so I was in a sorry state by the time I reached the house. My job entailed cleaning up after the servants, the butler and the maids, but I worked my way up to being in charge. When I left I went to work in a Spark Plug Factory in Putney, Surrey - KLGG. After I was married I worked in Preston Hospital Laundry and then went on to Tyne Brand Factory when I was widowed. When Spillers took over from Tyne Brand, the rate of pay was altered so that we got the same wages as the men.

I left school at 14 on Friday 15th December - I know the date because it was my birthday. In my first job I worked serving in a baker's shop from 7.30 am to 6 pm for 10/6d wages. At the start of the day we had to pack up the buns and deliver them to the cafes on the fish quay. Then we sold the rest of the buns in the shop. When the shop was closed on a Wednesday, we cleaned the boss's house for a half-a-crown. We had to the buy the clothes for the boss and his family and take the baby clothes to the laundry and back. We scrubbed the bakery floors and the shop floors and often whitewashed the back shop. The bakery was in Stephenson Street and I lived in Lynn Road, Billy Mill and I had to walk to work and back each day. We stayed for lunch and were allowed to eat a bun each. We swapped buns for Manley's crisps but if we wanted pies, we had to pay for them.

17

I had to go home for lunch that day, as the heat in the bakery made the tan run and I had streaks running down my legs - when I got home, mother thought it was distemper.

On my first day I wore a white overall and white ankle socks, and I had my hair in plaits. The other assistant insisted that I took off the socks and painted my legs with leg-tan. I had to go home for lunch that day, as the heat in the bakery made the tan run and I had streaks running down my legs - when I got home, mother thought it was distemper. I was persuaded to have my plaits cut off and have a half-crown Toni home-perm. When my father came home from sea, he didn't recognise me at first! When he did, I was walloped for cutting off my plaits! I loved working there - they baked the bread on the premises. I still correspond with the family owners. The eldest brother, Stan is now 90 and his wife, who had been a shop girl, is about 65. One of the brothers was in the Army and one was in the Air-force and when they came home on leave we were all invited to go and celebrate with the family.

Italians built Norham Road and our parents told us never to look at them. I wanted to work in a factory and we were taken from school to look at one with a view to a job. We had to walk down past the Italians and my mother was horrified when she found out. Factory work was well paid, but my father put his foot down and wouldn't allow me to take a job. My Grandma Rivers got the job at Hancock's Bakery for me. In those days you did as you were told and your job was picked for you.

I left school at 14. Three of us from the Dole started together at the Store (Co-op) Cleaners in Wallsend. The hours were from 7.30am to 5pm, and although I didn't like it I worked there for 3 years. I was the first one of the three to leave. I loved my next job - it was during the war years and during rationing - in a sweet shop. I worked there for 12 months and every time I weighed out a bag of sweets I put one in my mouth. My next job was as a barmaid in the Blyth and Tyne Pub in Stephenson Street. I worked at lunch-time and in the evenings for £3. 17s 0d. per week. I liked the regular crowd that came in. I met my husband there.

18

A lady came from the Charles Clay Factory to our school - she was a recruitment officer. She offered us training in Manchester for a month with a view to working in the factory. There was a family feud about this - as my parents disapproved of women working in factories. But I got my own way - as a friend and I both went with her mother to supervise us. So I became a machinist in a Clothing factory at age 14 for 5/- per week. I loved it and worked there for 9 months. Then I went as a trainee to Moore's Printers. One day I was asked to clean out the toilets, which were filthy and no brush was provided. I refused to put my hands in the toilets and was disciplined by the lady gaffer - A little old woman was the boss - she was a horrid woman - but the male gaffer who was nice offered to come with me when I was sent in for disciplining. My father made me hand in my notice as a result.

I then went on to a knitwear factory in Chirton Cottage. It was during the wartime - our boss, Mr. Hoffman was a German. The cottage had an orchard at the back and we used to steal apples for our lunch. I went on to be a hand finisher. The factory was by the bus station. I did invisible mending, and then overlocking. I loved machine work. My first rise was half a crown and the next rise was 7/6d. I thought I was rich - In those days you handed your wages over to your mother and given pocket money. I got half a crown pocket money. Mother put 1/- away for me in savings and I had 1/6d to spend on myself.

After School I attended Coulson's Commercial College. Firms rang them to offer employment. My first job was with Wolfes - a Jewish Firm- but I had to leave because the woman I worked with wore such overpowering perfume that I used to get dreadful headaches. I then worked in a poky upstairs office for a food distributor for hotels and shops - John Grant's of Low Friar Street in Newcastle. The war was just over then, but we got perks like dried egg, extra sugar, etc., as rationing was still in force.

I then went to Sun Electrical Company in Worswick Street as a Junior Typist. On my first day, the Senior Typist, who was responsible for the work from the top directors, didn't turn up for work. She left me on my own and I had to do typing work for the bosses and managers. I had so many letters to type that I didn't finish them and had to stay behind. I was so worried, but I got them all done. Just after that there was an epidemic of Asian Flu. I was the only one who didn't catch it and so I had to do the job of about 4 people at once. I did invoices, typing and answered the telephone, which was a headphone switchboard all at the same time. When the epidemic was over, I had a complete breakdown from exhaustion and had to be on the sick for 2 months.

I then became a Secretary for a branch of a London firm in Milburn House on the Quayside. The company made time switches for Street lamps, etc. It was really easy going after my last job. The boss was never in the office and so I used to invite my friends to come for lunch with me. As long as the work got done I could please myself. On a typical day when the boss was in the office, I used to go with him to meetings to take notes. We began by meeting a client in the Turks Head (opposite the Theatre Royal) for a drink, then lunch in the Clayton Street Hotel (where I drank Pimms No. 1) followed by a Cream Tea at the Royal Station Hotel and then home early. I got £7 per week for that job. My mum often got the bus to Newcastle and came to lunch and a look around the shops for an hour or two, but I still got all my work done.

20

Some of the customers were a bit hard to handle - one man from GEC offered to buy me a flat in Jesmond, but I told him where to go! Another man, who was quite high up in the Electricity Board was taken to lunch by my boss and I, as usual went to take notes. The meeting was very important as we needed his order. He sat next to me at the lunch table and he kept putting his hand on my leg - I thought hard before saying anything as I didn't want to jeopardise our chances of getting his order, but I couldn't stand for it any longer and I shouted at him: "Keep your hands to yourself or I'll slap you!" Everyone was very embarrassed, but we still won the order. I think he was afraid that his wife might find out. I loved it because I had set the office up to my own requirements and was more or less my own boss most of the time. I worked there until I got married.

I left school at 15. The Wednesday of my last week, Welch's Factory came into the school with an offer of 4 jobs. Eight of us applied and the interviews were on the next day, the Thursday. I was one of the lucky ones and I started on the following Monday at 7.30am. First of all I was asked my shoe size and I said I took size 5. I wondered what they wanted to know that for, but it turned out that everyone in the factory had to wear Clogs. The clogs were very uncomfortable - they were steel underneath and so were slippery on the warehouse floors - and I got blisters on my feet as my socks were quite thin. One of the drivers took pity on me and gave me his thick socks to wear! Of the four taken on 3 were needed to work in the factory, but I was taken to the warehouse to pack up the boxes to go onto the wagons. I worked there for about 6 months and when the next set of school-leavers arrived. The warehouse was staffed by boys only so I was moved onto a machine - feeding through the barley sugar to be sent abroad.

She had odd shoes, one green and one orange and one black stocking and the other leg bare and she had a broad Cockney accent.

One day Mr. Welch came to talk to the new starters and told us that there was a film star coming to visit the factory. We all had to wear our best uniforms and snood caps and I was picked to present a bouquet of flowers. The film star turned out to be Joan Dowling - a comedy actress - and when she arrived everybody burst out laughing at her. She had odd shoes, one green and one orange and one black stocking and the other leg bare and she had a broad Cockney accent. I was shaking as I handed her the flowers partly due to nerves and partly in case I laughed, but she had her photograph taken with all the machinists. During the tour she helped herself to sweets and had her mouth crammed full all the time.

A couple of months after that I was moved into the bottle wash - it was very noisy from the machines and you were constantly soaking wet. The job was to wash out all the empty bottles returned from shops. They were a nice crowd of girls to work with, but then the bottle wash became automated and we went back into the factory. I worked from 7.30am to 5 in the evenings with two nights overtime and Saturday mornings for a wage of £1. 1s 9d.

Before that, whilst I was at school, at about 13, I worked in Newtons Fish Shop on Tynemouth Road helping out - Even when I started at Welch's I kept that job on for a while. After I married I moved to the Tyne Brand Factory.

A lady came to our school to offer us jobs. I was taken on by Taylor Merrimaids. I left school on the Friday and started at the factory on the Monday morning. I was taken on as a sewing machinist, but we had to be trained first. We trained for a while using only paper and were not allowed near the material until we had mastered the machine. I think I earned around £20 per week of which I gave £5 board money to my mother. Out of the rest I had to buy everything I needed, including all my clothes. We did piece work at the factory, so the more you made, the more you could earn. I worked there for about two and a half years until I got married.

We all had to hand over our wages to the family and got pocket money back, but our clothes were bought for us, or home made. We were similar ages and so were dressed alike until we were in our teens. People thought that we were twins and on the occasions when we went out with our brother (he was 19 and we were about 4 years old) we were taken for his children. We got 6d each pocket money out of our wages.

I started work at the Tyne Brand Factory where I worked on the Paste Floor. There was a large table full of paste and we had to straighten up the tins and level off the tops and then stick on the parchment. After the process became automated we were paid off and I was sent to the Pop Factory. We had to wash the bottles and then the machines. We had to lift all the boxes ourselves and there were 12 bottles in every box - we were only 17 then. Magnus Purvis drove the horse and cart which took the pop round to be sold. I worked there for 2 years from 1947-48. I worked in the NAAFI in 1949 and got married in 1951. I went back to Tyne Brand for 12 months and then went to live in married quarters in Germany.

I was a supervisor when I left Tyne Brand - I was 58 and I got £70 per week plus bonuses. Most of the people in Shields didn't buy from Tyne Brand. They made Soup, steak, sandwich pastes and meats, but then Spillers took over the food production. Eventually they only made cat and dog food.

The Tyne Brand foods are still sold and have a good reputation now, but in those days people wouldn't buy them for the stories that went round about the factory floor - that the rubbish fell into the vats and was canned as well. We were terrified of the Tyne Brand girls.

It was the same in Wallsend - only it was the girls who worked for Haggies that frightened us - we crossed the road when we saw them coming out of work.

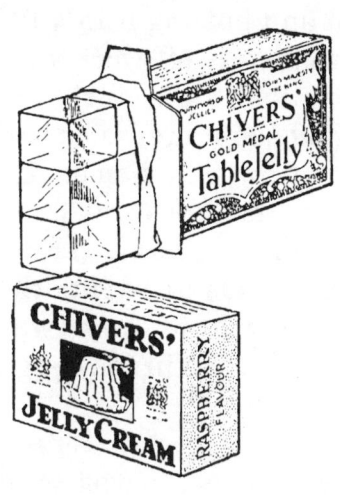

The stories that went around about Tyne Brand were all myth. The floor was spotlessly clean and the waste was put into swill-bins and given to the pig-man. We had to lift the huge soup buckets and take them to the machines - if you spilt any on the floor it had to be wiped up or it would be dangerously slippery. If anyone had an accident, they were immediately removed from the factory floor and taken to the Infirmary.

There was an old fish-wife who sold a bowl of fish - baked or fried herring - for 6d - she pushed a barrow through Cullercoats, Percy Main, Howdon and all around the town. There was also Mrs. Todd from Shields who sold prawns at 24 for 1d. At Dove Cottages in Cullercoats the fishwives sold prawns, fish and shellfish from their doorsteps. They wore Black dresses, white pinnies and bonnets.

We had a bit of fun but nobody got hurt .....

We had a bit of fun but nobody got hurt .....

I remember being sent for a reel of Tartan Thread - I felt stupid when I caught on to the joke.

When I was 14 years old I was as green as grass and as a prank I was sent to the boss's office for a 'long stand'. I kept knocking on the door but no-one answered. I was there for ages before I realised that that was my 'long stand'.

I remember being sent for a reel of Tartan Thread - I felt stupid when I caught on to the joke.

I was sent for a wire-netting oil can.

One of the lads put me in the dough cupboard at the bakery and I was covered in flour. I got my own back by buying some Boniment laxative chewing gum and putting it in a PK gum packet. He ate some and was off work with diarrhoea the next day - his wife rang work and said that she was very worried about him as he had dirtied himself on the bus on the way home! He retaliated when ages afterwards I was walking past the dough cupboard and I felt a hand cover my mouth so I could not scream. I was lifted into the dough cupboard and the machine fork was switched on - I was lifted up and down in the dough by the mechanical grab.

I was put in the 'pickle-vat' - where I was dyed orange, and then hosed down.

During
The War

I went to Ralph Gardner School during the war and when the sirens went we didn't know whether to run to school or run home. We had an Anderson air-raid shelter at home. My father was the air-raid warden and stood outside the shelter in his tin hat after he had rounded us all up. We had to take blankets into the shelter. Sometimes it was only about 10 minutes before the All Clear sounded, but it could be up to two hours at a time in the shelter. I remember the houses being bombed on the site where Meadowell School is now. I remember Wilkinsons Pop Factory being bombed, but we weren't allowed to go near the site.

I remember when the siren first went on Sunday Sept. 3rd, 1939 at 11 am., but it was a false alarm or a test, everyone ran into their shelters. When the war broke out I was working in the Sparking Plug factory making parts for the aeroplanes, and we all had to run outside into the stone shelters provided at the factory, and stay there until all clear sounded.

25

We worked all hours and weekends during the war, but after the war and we went home there was a lot of damage. There was a cemetery at the back of the factory and those who were killed and not identified were put into lime-pits in the cemetery. The factory was in Putney, in London, so there was a lot of damage around about. The war was over when I came home to Shields. The memories were awful. We only got home once a year for holidays. I was about 19 or 20 when I went into the factory after I left service. I married my husband at 21, he was in the army.

I remember standing in a queue for stockings for about four hours in the freezing cold, and lost the stockings on my way home. They must have dropped out of my hand without me noticing, because my hands were numb from the cold.

We were bombed out in Railway Terrace and moved to Coburg Terrace and I went to King Edwards School. We lived one street away from Wilkinsons Shelter and both families on either side of our house during the bombings were killed in that shelter. There were complete families wiped out all along Tynemouth Road. We didn't use that shelter as we had one in the back yard - it was like a stone wash-house converted with beds and blankets. Father was in the mine sweepers and so we didn't see a great deal of him during the war. The sound of the sirens made me feel sick - the memories of that time are horrible. After that I went to Linskill School, I lost a lot of friends - there were only three people left in my class after the Wilkinson disaster, 40 children out of the class had died and we were sent home from school, I had to collect my brother as the school was closed that morning, and as we came home the siren sounded again as we got to King Street. We saw an aeroplane flying low and we had to lie flat on the ground until he passed as he was shooting at everyone. We never went up that street again.

We always worried about what was happening to my father. They are times you never want to go back to or think about. It was wonderful when it was over.

I went to St. Aidans School and when the war started, if there was an air-raid we were sent home and had to go into the air-raid shelter. We were lucky to avoid the bombings although we lived beside a railway siding. Some bombs fell in the fields around, which shook the place a little, but no major damage was done. My friends all lived in South Shields and I went over there on the ferry one Saturday.

I was out quite late and was coming home at about 8 pm when the sirens sounded and the ferry was stopped in the middle of the river. Bombs were dropping all around and we were frightened and soaking wet. My dad was furious and I wasn't allowed to go to South Shields again for quite some time. I was glad when it was all over.

For a while we didn't go to school at all because they were converting shelters inside the school, but then we went half day only. Half of the children went in the morning and the other half in the afternoon, so we had some spare time each day. On the Sunday morning (3rd September 1939) I was in the paper shop as usual, sent for papers and the sweets and lemonade for after Sunday Dinner, and I was waiting to be served and the next thing my dad was behind me in the shop to drag me home. On the first day there was so much panic. You would have thought that the skies had opened and that they were going to drop all the bombs at once there and then, everyone was in such a state. I think the thing that sticks in my memory most of all were the smoke screens which hung along the main roads.

With no lights and a small torch, ten to one you would walk into one - more people I knew were hurt by that than anything else. But my father was working in the shipyards - at Swans - and they worked all hours. We used to say that they had more time in than the rats! When he did come home, he had a quick meal and then the sirens would sound and he was back out on air-raid duty.

> *I remember one particular night there was one woman saying her prayers in the corner, another one calling them names and a third one putting rollers into her daughters hair, the faster the bombs dropped the quicker she put the rollers in - we had to have some humour as well as the sad times.*

> *My mother shoved us to the ground and mother thought we had had it - but she said: "As long as I've got my bairns with me it's all right".*

At home we didn't have a garden and so we had one of the brick shelters in the yard for upstairs and downstairs neighbours. Some of the neighbouring families used to come into our shelter for company rather than sit in their own shelters alone. I remember one particular night there was one woman saying her prayers in the corner, another one calling them names and a third one putting rollers into her daughters hair, the faster the bombs dropped the quicker she put the rollers in - we had to have some humour as well as the sadtimes.

For all we lived beside the shipyards we were lucky not to lose anyone from the family. Because the shipyards weren't hit we used to call it "Von Hunters"! They hit the railway line, but never the shipyard. One plane came down into the river - we saw him flying very low and the pilot parachuted out. On VJ night I was in the Theatre Royal, in Newcastle and the show was stopped to make the announcement. Greeta Gint was in the show - we had a great time in Newcastle after that.

I remember the bomb falling on the grass where Meadowell School is now, and bombed out 6 houses on Waterville Road. Fortunately no-one was killed but one lad was badly injured. We used to go in the shelter with the lady from downstairs who had a big family and we used to help to carry her children into the shelter for her. We had a singsong in the shelter to keep up spirits: 'Run Rabbit Run' and 'When the Lights Go On Again'. My father was the Air Raid Warden. One night we went to the Boro and we were walking up Waterville Road with our mother when a German plane came over. My mother shoved us to the ground and mother thought we had had it - but she said: "As long as I've got my bairns with me it's all right". In Peartree there was a small field behind the houses, and a pilot came over there so low that you could have waved to him, but I didn't - I ran instead!

I remember VJ Day - my friend's brother in law was lost in the Navy and when we heard that the war was over we ran into the street in celebration but her sister was looking out of the window with tears running down her face. She said: "I haven't got my husband, but at least I've got my son". We all went to Lawson street and we had bonfires by the docks and we went out and had a great time with some merchant navy lads from London. The next night they took us to the Howards and we saw "Springtime".

I went to a friends house who had no air-raid shelter and used to use the cupboard under the stairs as a shelter. I stayed there to sleep when her husband was away in the army to keep her company. She woke me from a sound sleep one night to tell me that there had been an air raid warning and we had to go into the cupboard in the early hours of the morning. The next morning at about 9.30am, the neighbour from next door came in and asked why we were still in the cupboard. We said we were waiting for the all clear to sound. She said it had already sounded at about 2.30 that morning - so we must have missed the air raid warning and gone into the cupboard after the all clear had sounded!

The shop where I worked later on, Hancocks, we used to go down there to get the bread, and one of the girls who I was friendly with, said: "We've got a date tonight with some GIs". My friend was dying to get a date with a GI, but I didn't know what a GI was! She said a GI was American and I said I'd never had one of those before. They laughed at me for that.

We went to the Howard with them and there were nine of us all sitting in a row chewing gum! I thought of what my parents would say if they could see me there and I made an excuse to go to the toilet, and went home. There was a knock at the door later on and I was ready for bed in my nightdress with my hair in rags and it was the girls with these GIs. The look on my mothers face - I thought I was going to be put into a home, she was furious - she asked me what I had been doing. I told her I had done nothing but chew their chewing gum!

Two of the girls married GIs. I was in the factory then and we still had clothing rationing. My mother had bought me a horrible dress covered in sequins and I hated it - I gave it to my friend, Ethel, as a going away present - everyone clubbed together and gave them clothes to take away. She took away better clothes than we were wearing at the time and years later we got letters thanking us for helping them out. I thought that American families all slept together in one bed and told my friend that I was glad I hadn't married a GI as I would hate to share a bed with 13 other people!

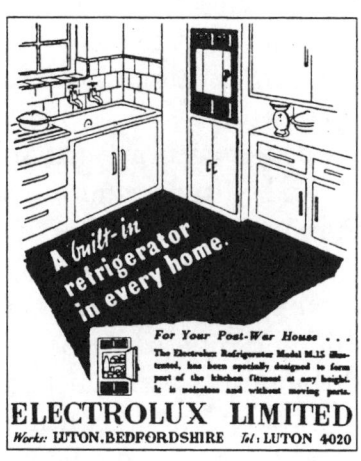

My brother Stan was in the merchant navy. We had a dog called Rover who used to sit on the top of the stairs when the lads were due home on leave, as if he knew they were coming. He used to sit there and howl. My brother was only 16 then and they had been Torpedoed and came home at about 2.30 am in the morning. Usually their ship had carried guns and ammunition to the troops at Dunkirk - on the beaches, but their orders had been changed and they were loaded with foodstuffs and papers when they were hit by the torpedo. They were really lucky to have had the cargo changed or they would have been killed. I had had a dream a couple of night before where I saw him sitting on deck drinking coffee. I asked him what he had been doing at the time and he said he had been sitting drinking coffee on deck with the lads when the torpedo hit.

My other brother Bill was in the Royal Navy - he used to entertain the troops. Unfortunately they never got home at the same time on leave. My older brother John was in the army but he went on the hospital ships. We loved them coming home, but we hated seeing them leave again, my mother took it worse than any of us.

My mother used to cry her eyes out when my brother went away. There were three girls and my brother. We used to have parties when he came home - no drink, but we still enjoyed ourselves.

Two of my brothers were in the forces before the war. One was home on leave and was called up again straight away. My other brother was in Cairo and was shipped home to fight. They were both taken Prisoners of War - one in Dunkirk and the other somewhere else. My eldest brother was in Dunkirk as POW for about five years - his son was nearly six when he was allowed home. The youngest was not married, and had been a POW for years and I had not seen him since I was about 14, but when I answered the door and saw the soldier standing there, I just yelled and all the neighbours came out to see what was the matter. I recognised him straight away.

My father was on a Mine sweeper with my cousin and they were torpedoed and lifted ashore at Sheerness. My grandmother had to look after us because my mother had to go there. All the family were in the Army or the Merchant Navy and out of my aunts family of four lads only one came back, all the rest were killed. All the family was touched by death. Everyone waited at the Central Station in Newcastle for their loved ones coming home from war. We blame the war for families being split up and being strangers. My cousin went away when his wife was expecting and had a grown up son when he came home - he never got attached to the family after that - they were always distant.

I was always being sent to Lloyds Hailing Station with a list of ships to see if any of the family were coming home. I remember the number for the Lloyds Hail Station - North Shields 32. They all came to my mothers house for weddings and christenings. I hated going to the station to see them off - they all used to sing Auld Lang Syne and now I can't bear that song as it brings back bad memories of those days.

Managing In Wartime

Ration books were like small coupons. You got: 2oz butter, 1 rasher of bacon and one egg per week. Powdered egg was used for cooking things like Yorkshire pudding and cakes. The buzz went round whenever there were supplies to the shops. Eggs were so scarce that by the time you got them you were due about a dozen each, even though you were only allowed one a week. Eggs were a luxury and so were bananas. The queues for everything were miles long.

Once I was on a train with two girls who had a banana each. They didn't know what to do with them, but as one bit into her banana the train went into the tunnel. She shouted to her sister: "Don't eat the banana it'll make you go blind!"

If you were pregnant you were given a green ration book which entitled you to a banana a week. Once I was on a train with two girls who had a banana each. They didn't know what to do with them, but as one bit into her banana the train went into the tunnel. She shouted to her sister: "Don't eat the banana it'll make you go blind!" During the war there were no lights on the trains. You got tea, butter and cheese, but you had to take a ration book to get them and they were in use after the war until supplies built up. Clothing coupons were in force too. A dressmaker in St. George's Road used to make our clothes as it was cheaper than buying them.

My mother used a dressmaker for our clothes and we used to share the coupons so that everyone got the same patterned dress. Once there was a flaw in the material and I got the dress with the flawed fabric and had to keep a cardigan on. We didn't get many new clothes, but we got a lot handed down and altered to fit. I was sent to the queues by my mother - I was always in different queues. Bacon pieces were worth waiting for and potatoes. Once at school, two girls who had lost their fathers in the war were given bananas and they were afraid to eat them. The teacher had to show them how to peel and eat them.

Only one thing I really hated about rationing was when you couldn't get lard, my mother used to take me on a Saturday morning to queue up for tripe - at a place in Coach Lane. I hated the smell - you used to have to have a bath after standing for hours in the queue in the shop because of the smell. With each pound of tripe you got a half a pound of lard. I can't look at tripe now, or pigs trotters.

My mother used to buy cow heel - to make pies, and pigs feet. We had the radio on all the time - it was the only way you could get any news at all, newspapers were just local news because everything was censored. There was a lot they didn't tell you, My brother often had his orders changed, but he wasn't allowed to pass it on to us.

She had the back door open and she went to answer the front door, and when she came back a cat had got in and taken the sausages off the table.

The Co-op was at the top of the street, and someone told us that they had got stocks of butter in. There were so many people in the Co-op for the butter that I was pressed up against the counter and had a pain in my stomach. I eventually got the butter, and another time I was sent for meat - I was given a half shoulder of lamb, which was mostly bone and fat. When my mother dropped it onto the plate, the plate cracked in half. Another time my mother had bought pork sausages. She had the back door open and she went to answer the front door, and when she came back a cat had got in and taken the sausages off the table.

We used to go to the Co-op for rations. They took out the coupons and marked the card each time you went. I had a friend who worked in a fruit shop and so I got some fruit from her.

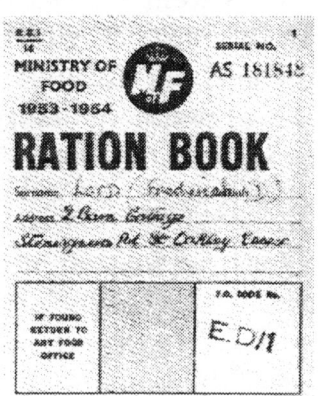

As long as you had tea you were all right. There was always a pot of tea on the table and you took a flask of tea into the shelter with you. You got powdered milk, but if you didn't get it right it floated on the top of the tea - it was revolting. People had to grow their own vegetables and if you got a little bit of meat you always had to fill up with vegetables.

I used to have to go with my aunt to Cooks pork butchers on Saville Street and stand in the queue from 7.30 am until 9.30 am until the shop opened to be given half a pound of sausage, a quarter of pease pudding and a quarter of black pudding. He gave all of his customers the same however big their families, so that everyone had some and no-one was left with nothing. We had a big family and mother skinned the sausages and make sausage rolls for everyone to make the half a pound of sausage go round.

Do you remember the British Restaurants ? - they served a meal and a sweet with a cup of tea - it isn't many years since the one in Gateshead closed down. Especially for people on their own, it was a way to eke out the rations and save some money. The meals were very cheap and there was soup as a starter when it was available. They used whatever there was available to make a cheap meal, but there was always a pudding served and a cup of tea. It cost about 1/6d for a three course meal.

The sirens were on top of the Rex Cinema in North Shields. If you were in the street when the siren sounded, you were ushered into the nearest shelter by the Air Raid Wardens. A neighbour would take you in, or you could go into the big public shelters. At night you went into your own shelter and the children were encouraged to sing to pass the time and keep out the noise. You may have to be in the shelter for a couple of hours.

34

We were always given to understand that the Sirens came from the river on the ships.

I remember when a plane sneaked in during the day. When the sirens went we were in the street and a lady dragged us into her shelter. The plane was machine-gunning the streets. At that age, we didn't realise the danger, we took it all as fun. I remember the bomb dropping on the Ridges Infant School. I wouldn't get up when the siren went off because usually there was not much happening, but that night my mother shouted up the stairs for us to get out of bed, the slates were falling off the roof - we went into the coal house under the stairs. That is the only time I remember fear during the war - most of the time it was just excitement. We collected shrapnel as souvenirs. My dad was a Warden and he always stood outside our shelter.

In 1941, machinery from the top floor at the Wilkinsons Factory, fell onto the shelter below which crushed the people in there - it was not the blast which killed them.

Wartime Entertainment

I was only 10 when the war started: We still went to our dances at the Mem. in Wallsend, a hop on Jackson Street, St. Joseph's Church, Memorial, Miners, Plaza, the Albion. Life was not changed too much, war became a way of life, we still went to the pictures and dances. Towards the end of the war we were teenagers and we got used to it apart from the blackouts - it was very like Ireland must be today - we just carried on. We were frightened and nervous, but we will never forget the day the war ended. Everyone drew their curtains open and turned on the lights. It was very bright and the street lights all came on. We lit a bonfire on Waterville Road and celebrated, dancing and singing - doing the conga up and down the street.

I wasn't much of a dancer, but we still went to dances, for a bit of carry on with the lads. Friday night was Amami night - we always washed our hair on a Friday with Amami Shampoo.

My dad didn't allow us to go to dances at St. Josephs, but we went to dances at the drill hall in Tynemouth - that's where I learned to dance - with the boys from our school. I went to a youth club at the YWCA with my sisters. Most of the dances served soft drinks and tea. The Plaza and the Drill Hall were the only places with bars. We didn't need a drink - we just went to enjoy the dancing and the company.

I wasn't old enough to go to the dances, but I went to the church youth clubs. The Mem was the first dance I went to at the end of the war - a sailor who had had too much to drink was thrown over the top of the stairwell and was killed - I never told my parents or they wouldn't allow me to go back. I went to the pictures at the Boro, Ritz, Queens, Tyne, they're all Bingo Halls now! The Queens was very dirty, you had to have a bath when you got home. The Borough had stone steps in the Gods to sit on, it was very cheap. We used to get into the Ritz through the toilet windows at the back so we never had to pay. Kids these days think these pranks had never been thought up but we had done them all in our day.

At the matinees we used to sing "the Mystery Riders" theme tune, whilst we ate our penny lucky bags.

My mother went to see the play "Dracula" at the Theatre Royal, Theatre Place, North Shields and afterwards they went on to a dance at Albion Road. The actor playing Dracula turned up at the dance but no-one would dance with him as they were all afraid of him.

The first owner of the Theatre Royal was Arthur Jefferson - Stan Laurel's father. It is said that Stan Laurel first acted on the stage of the Theatre Royal in North Shields. The family lived in Dockwray Square, my aunt lived next door to them, she worked for a Doctor there.

At the Boro Cinema there was the "posh end" and the "pit end" - as it was known - had wooden forms or benches in rows - that's where we used to sit. We always came out covered in flea-bites. The picture always broke down half way through and we stamped our feet to make it work again.

Once we went to the Picture Hall and I had to leave early as I was feeling ill. The Picture Hall was bombed that night and everyone inside was killed. We were very lucky to have been saved.

The Central Palace on Saville Street was a comedy theatre - it was really small inside. The piano player, Billy Ternent became a famous band leader.

We always came out covered in flea-bites. The picture always broke down half way through and we stamped our feet to make it work again.

Getting Married And Setting Up Home

I met my husband at the youth club at the Co-op in Wallsend. We got engaged before he went to do his two years National Service in the Army. My mother was in poor health and her doctor advised her to move to a smaller house on the coast. She swapped houses and got a one bedroomed flat. There was no room for me at the new house and so I moved in with my fiancé's mother. I thought I might as well be married and get the allowances so I rang him up at the army camp one evening and told him he had to get leave for the 7th July so that we could be married. We hired a hall and had two bridesmaids and he wore his army uniform and so did the best man. We could not have a honeymoon as he only had a weekend pass. We had about 100 guests and a band. My first night was spent at my mother in law's house and she brought us breakfast in bed the next morning.

We collected for our bottom drawer. When his sister moved out of her house, she gave us a lot of her furniture and we moved into a house in Chirton Grange. Most of the other residents were in the same boat and we all helped each other out. When we were waiting for the pay on a Thursday night we combined all the food we had left, and shared it out to feed all the families.

I had a white wedding - my mother was dead, but my mother-in-law wanted it. I had stale tea-cake for my reception buffet at the Park Hotel. We went to a boarding house in Scarborough for our honeymoon and we had to walk miles for fish and chips in the pouring rain as we were starving when we got there. We still had our ration books in single names and so everyone guessed we were a honeymoon couple. The weather improved after a while.

We had rooms in Alma Place and a shared kitchen. We got rooms in Huntingdon Place in Tynemouth and we were able to use some of our own furniture. We then moved to a three bedroomed house in Chirton Grange, beside Joyce, in Tintern Crescent. Then we moved to Aldwich Drive. We went to a place in Dock Road every so often and took old woollies to the Rag Shop that was there, in prams. When we got money for them, we used to go to the bakery and have a bean feast. It was all give and take then, and we pooled our food resources to feed the children.

I met my husband in the pub where I was working. He was in uniform then. My father thought I was too young, but we got married. We couldn't live in, as there was no room at home, but we eventually got a house. My husband went into the pits after he left the army. We always helped each other out and the neighbours shared food out. I had nine children to feed. I never drank although I worked in a pub, but I used to go to the pictures. I was married 47 years, before he died.

My parents weren't at my wedding. I lived with my mother and then I got a house in Bridge Road South. That house was my pride and joy. I was given a three piece and a dining set. I bought a new bed. We had no carpet, but lino. After 7 years my marriage broke up. I had my two daughters though. When we had no money, the lady across the road at the fish shop used to let us have our supper and pay when we got our wages. We had no TV only a radio, but we sat and talked for hours. I had five children in my second marriage.

Everyone helped each other out - we shared our rations. We were sometimes so hard up that you had to swallow your pride and ask the neighbours and family for help to buy food. Ration books were still used for years after the war - as late as the early fifties.

My brother got a house which was on the site of the Wilkinson disaster. The council were called in to investigate subsidence under the house as the walls were cracked. Cement was pumped under the house to try and hold it up, but the subsidence was still there. His family was moved out, but another family were housed there after that and the house is still standing. My brother said that he could hear noises coming from the foundations. He found a signet ring in his garden once whilst he was digging. He loved the house, but the memory of the disaster made it very sad, very tragic, as so many people died.

I moved into Elsdon Street in North Shields, with only one bedroom and a small living room with a range. It was a tenement building. The one bedroom was enormous, it took 26 rolls of wallpaper. I called it my "ballroom". The range was full of beetles and I asked the council to come and sort it out. I was given a Triplex stove which had to go into the bedroom. The two girls had two single beds and we had a double bed in that room. I moved back into the street we lived in as children. A three bedroomed house in Cherrytree - which we moved into using a barrow to take the furniture.

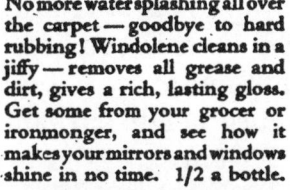

I had all of my children, except for the last one, at home. I lived there until it was renovated when I was moved into a four bedroomed house in Waterville Road. I carried my furniture through the gardens to my new house. It had central heating. The Ridges became the Meadowell Estate when the renovation began. I loved my home and had no trouble, but my sister's house was broken into several times.

I moved from East Howdon and I was very wary of moving onto the Ridges Estate after hearing bad stories. The 3-bedroomed flat was lovely, but the lady upstairs was quite a tartar. We moved to a 4-bedroomed in Prestbury - all my family brought their girlfriend and boyfriends to the house and they all brought their records and played them loudly. I lived on the estate for many years and had no trouble at all.

The first house we had was in Tintern and was a 3 bedroomed house. The kitchen was modern. My neighbour was atrocious. We used to make our own amusement. We had card nights with pie and pea suppers. The community centre on the estate needed help with the youth club and I volunteered. We all got on very well and left our children with neighbours while we went shopping or went to work. My mother-in-law never looked after the children while we went out. We shared a path with a younger family and we all helped each other out. I had a happy life.

I had three sons. My third was born in December after I moved to Tintern. I had a dog - she was the first one in the street and thought she owned the place. We lived there for about 12 years and then I moved into a bigger house in Kirton Park Terrace to take in my mother who had Alzheimer's disease. Two of my sons joined the services and later my mother died. The house was too big and so we moved to Seaton Delaval, but we had to give up the house when my husband suffered bad health. The council re-housed us in Cramlington, which we hated, and after 8 years and my husband in worse health - we then got a furnished flat in North Shields and joined the Council Waiting List.

... And Then We Moved To Royal Quays

I had a lovely house on Meadow Well but I had so many break-ins, so I had no regrets about moving on to Royal Quays. I had lived there so long, but my house was vandalised so many times that I was sick of living there. The best thing that happened to me was moving here.

I was delighted when I got a bungalow. I now go out and have lots of friends. I used to live in a furnished flat, and previously Cramlington.

I lived on Meadow Well and then moved to Trust Houses on Howdon Road. When stolen cars were going round the estate, I had no rest and had to be up early to get to work. I was rejected at first for a bungalow, but eventually got a 2 bedroomed house. I was the first tenant on the estate. We moved in on 14th December two years ago. I never regret it for a minute, as I never went out and now I'm with nice neighbours and a nice crowd at the Community Centre.

It was a life saver for me. I had lost my husband and I'd lost touch with North Shields people. I was at the bus stop with a total stranger and she asked me to go for coffee. I love the Community Centre.

I lived in a big house on Prestbury Road. I wanted to move from the Ridges and stuck out for a Bungalow on Royal Quays, with my daughter. I was delighted when I got a bungalow here, and I'm never in now. My daughter had to sign a paper to say that if anything happened to me she would move out.

I lived in Elmwood Road, which was Prestbury Road. I didn't have much bother but I stuck out to get a Bungalow or Sheltered Home, and when the Northern Housing offered me this bungalow, I was pleased. We all help each other like real neighbours and it is a real community - we have some good laughs.

Everyone had their ups and downs. My house was modernised. I had an outside toilet on the veranda and a Triplex stove. My bedroom at the rear of the house was made smaller and used to make the kitchen and toilet smaller. Some of the houses were over-run with mice. My house was pulled down and eventually I was given a Bungalow at Royal Quays. Now, the Northern Housing Association insist on 150 points before you can qualify for a Royal Quays Bungalow.

I was in my house on Waterville Road about 22 years and I moved with mixed feelings. The house was too big after the family had grown up and left. I had a bit of a fight to get a bungalow, but through ill-health I was awarded enough points to be able to move onto the Royal Quays. It's the best thing I ever did, we get out and socialise with our neighbours at the Centre. I had previously never got out in the evenings but now I have a new lease of life.

We built the community centre up from nothing and it's now quite successful. We got our Bingo Club about a year ago. We couldn't live without the Community Centre. We are going to the Pantomime at Christmas and we had a day out in Seahouses. I've really started to live since I came to live here.

When we had our day out at Seahouses - we took the Priory bus and went around the gift shops and had a meal. We went to Holy Island and tasted the mead. The Community Centre funds paid for the trip and we had a great time.

We had a Jumble Sale to raise funds for the centre. We had D-day celebrations and a dance and sang all the old songs. We would die without our club. On a Sunday we have a church service at the Community Centre - all the families come and some of the children read the lesson.

Bingo is on a Monday and Thursday, Wednesday and Friday is the youth club for the children.

We had Mosaic and Art Classes - we get notices through the door to keep us informed of what's going on. In the winter we like to come to the centre, just across the road. Handicrafts keep us occupied.

We are going to the Theatre Royal to the Pantomime and we are having a Christmas Party in the Community Centre as well.

The children always shout hello to us as they go past our houses. They come at Halloween and for school sponsors. We get on very well with the children - there is no trouble. They polish the play area to keep it clean. They pick up rubbish from the park. The children round here are very good and there is not usually any trouble from the ones down this end of the Estate. Our streets are very quiet most of the time.

We were lucky enough to get housed in Royal Quays. It has given me a new lease of life as I never got out at all before I moved here and now I'm never in.

I love my neighbours at Royal Quays, it's just like old times.

All the neighbours in the Royal Quays are very close, we are all friends and it reminds us of the times when we were children.